A Chef

by Douglas Florian

Greenwillow Books New York

Grateful acknowledgments to:
Peter Hoffman, Susan Rosenfeld, and David Wurth of The Savoy;
Lello Arpaia and Julio Salina of Scarlatti

Watercolor paints and pen and ink
were used for the full-color art.
The text type is Bryn Mawr.
Copyright © 1992
by Douglas Florian

Greenwillow Books,
a division of William
Morrow & Company, Inc.,
1350 Avenue of the Americas,
New York, NY 10019.
Printed in Hong Kong
by South China Printing
Company (1988) Ltd.

First Edition
10 9 8 7 6 5 4 3 2 1

Library of Congress Cataloging-in-Publication Data
Florian, Douglas.
A chef / by Douglas Florian.
p.   cm.
Summary:
Demonstrates how different
types of chefs work with
food and describes
some of the utensils
that they use.
ISBN 0-688-11108-4 (trade).
ISBN 0-688-11109-2 (lib.)
1. Cooks—Juvenile literature.
2. Cookery—Juvenile literature.
[1. Cooks.   2. Cookery.
3. Occupations.]   I. Title.
TX652.5.F59   1992
641.5'023—dc20
91-29545   CIP   AC

Pour mon petit chou, Marie

A chef works with food.

Early in the morning she shops at the market.

At the restaurant she checks deliveries

and plans the day's menu.

Before the restaurant opens, the chef
and her assistants prepare food.
One assistant washes the fruits and vegetables

and cuts them on a chopping board.

Another assistant trims the fat off meats, bones chickens,

and cleans fish.

Veal is cut into portions called cutlets, and pounded tender.

Potatoes are peeled, cut, and boiled.

The chef starts a stock for soup, stews, and sauces.
She boils meat bones, carrots, and onions in a big pot.

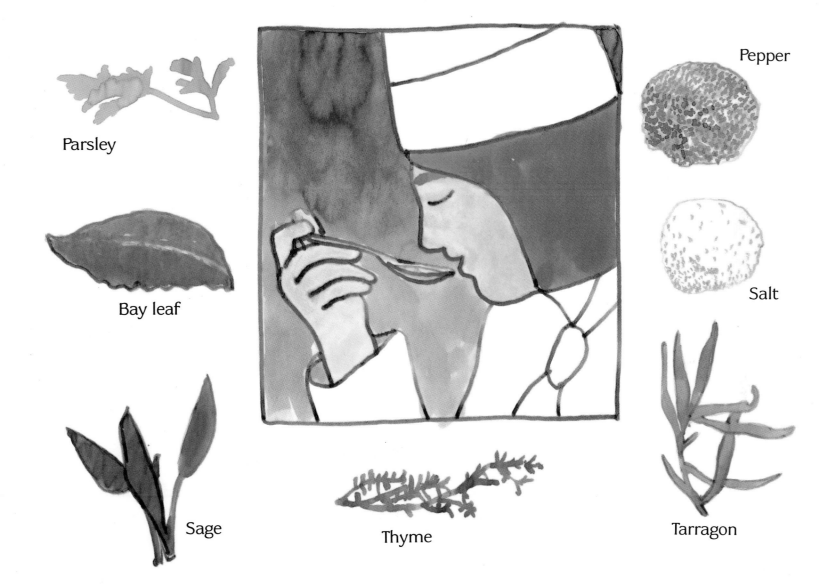

Parsley

Bay leaf

Sage

Thyme

Pepper

Salt

Tarragon

She seasons the stock with herbs and spices
and tests it by smell and taste.

A stew is cooked with stock, beef, onions, tomatoes, and potatoes.

Chickens are roasted in the oven.

The pastry chef makes deep-dish blueberry pies.

She washes fresh blueberries.

Then she adds flour and sugar.

She grates nutmeg and lemon peel.

And she mixes everything together.

She puts the mixture
into buttered ceramic cups.

She folds rolled dough over the cups
and cuts vents with a knife.

She glazes the tops with egg yolks
and sprinkles on sugar.

She bakes the pies twenty minutes,
and they're done!

She also mixes chocolate icing for a cake.

Now the restaurant is open.
The waiters bring in orders from the customers.

The chef and her assistants do last-minute cooking.
Pasta is boiled, then rinsed and drained in a colander.

The veal cutlets are cooked in a frying pan.

Fish is cooked on a grill

and served with vegetables.

The plates are picked up by a waiter

and served to the customers.

In restaurants...

and schools...

in hotels

in hospitals

in the military

at catered parties

and wherever many people eat...

a chef works with food.

A CHEF'S UTENSILS

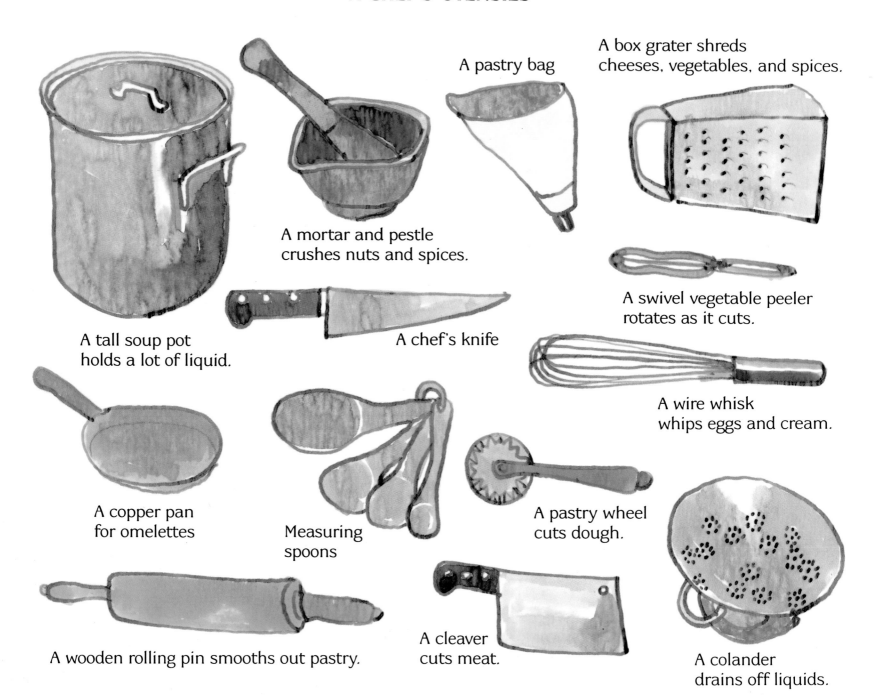

A pastry bag

A box grater shreds
cheeses, vegetables, and spices.

A mortar and pestle
crushes nuts and spices.

A swivel vegetable peeler
rotates as it cuts.

A tall soup pot
holds a lot of liquid.

A chef's knife

A wire whisk
whips eggs and cream.

A copper pan
for omelettes

Measuring
spoons

A pastry wheel
cuts dough.

A wooden rolling pin smooths out pastry.

A cleaver
cuts meat.

A colander
drains off liquids.